STUDYING VOCABULARY II

 PRESTWICK HOUSE, INC.

"Everything for the English Classroom!"

P.O. 246
Cheswold, DE 19936
1-800-932-4593
www.prestwickhouse.com
ISBN 1-58049-252-5

Revised January, 2002

To The Student

We have entitled our book *Studying Vocabulary* because we believe at some point in a school career each student must sit down and work at committing selected words and their definitions to memory. One of the purposes of this book and the available testing program is to encourage you to learn to do so.

Of course, anyone could memorize any word and its definition for the short term, but we want these words to stay with you for the rest of your life, so we have done the following:

- We have chosen high-frequency words that are generally found in everyday reading material and in the speech of the average person. In this way, your learning of these words, and definitions should be reinforced and made easier.

- In the event that you do not read very much, however, we have taken a second step. All of the quizzes in the testing program are cumulative. Each week you will be asked to identify the definitions of the new words *plus* various review words from previous lessons. Therefore, it is important from the outset that you study and pay attention to all the words, because they will be included in the following lessons.

TABLE OF CONTENTS

Page

LESSON ONE

Exercise I //

In your own words, write a brief definition for as many words on the list as you can. Then correct and/or complete the lesson by using the mini-dictionary in the back of this book.

1. ascend
2. audacity
3. casual
4. descend
5. emit
6. glance
7. illusion
8. literate
9. pier
10. pigment
11. scandalous
12. scold
13. thrash
14. void
15. whimper

Exercise II //

From the list of words, fill in the blanks to make complete sentences. Some words may have to be changed in form to fit the sentence by using plurals or adding "ed," "ly," "ing," etc.

1. The five-year-old was happy to start kindergarten, but his leaving left a(n) _____ in his mother's day.

2. A frowning _____ from the teacher made the students behave.

3. The fireman put up his ladder to _____ to the third floor.

4. Although a few people wore suits, it was a(n) _____ party.

5. The airplane was too high and had to _____ ten thousand feet to equalize the pressure.

6.   Because Joe was not _____, he could not read the directions.

7.   The Senator's _____ affair caused his defeat.

8.   The burning rays of the sun can harm the _____ of your skin.

9.   Her soft voice gave the _____ of helplessness.

10.   When surprised, the bird _____ a loud squawk.

11.   The lifeguard had to _____ the children who were running around the diving board.

12.   The puppy began to _____ from fear as the veterinarian examined him.

13.   The feverish child started to _____ about on the bed.

14   Mike had the _____ to challenge his father's decision.

15.   The yacht was securely tied at the _____ .

Exercise III

After studying the roots, prefixes, and suffixes, try to define the following words without using a dictionary. We have done the first one for you to get you started.

> The prefix *in* means "not"
> The suffix *able, ible* means "able" or "capable"
> The root *cred* means "believe"
> The root *aud* means "hear"
> The root *vid, vis* means "see"

1.   credible - able to be believed
2.   incredible -
3.   audible -
4.   inaudible -
5.   visible -
6.   invisible -
7.   If your television no longer has any audio, what has it lost? _____ .

LESSON TWO

Exercise I //

In your own words, write a brief definition for as many words on the list as you can. Then correct and/or complete the lesson by using the mini-dictionary in the back of this book.

1. accessible
2. acute
3. adamant
4. antisocial
5. apprehensive
6. bizarre
7. clement
8. combatant
9. console
10. curt
11. forlorn
12. horrify
13. meager
14. smug
15. unruly

Exercise II //

From the list of words, fill in the blanks to make complete sentences. Some words may have to be changed in form to fit the sentence by using plurals or adding "ed," "ly," "ing," etc.

1. The provisions were _____, especially for such a large crowd.

2. After he won, he had such a(n) _____ look on his face that it made me mad.

3. The crowd was so _____ that the police were summoned.

4. Do not let him _____ you with his crazy ghost stories.

5. He is so _____ that he immediately goes upstairs if anyone comes to the house to visit.

6. His manner was so _____that I gave up trying to talk to him.

7. After Bill left her, Joan had such a(n) _____ look on her face we all felt sorry for her.

8. The temperature was unusually _____ for January.

9. The campsite was _____ only by boat.

10. We were _____ about going into that part of the city after dark.

11. The pain in Jack's arm was not _____ but more like a dull ache.

12. The judge was _____ in his decision to clear the courtroom.

13. His behavior was so _____ that most people avoided him.

14. Marcy tried to _____ her heartbroken friend.

15. The boys sized each other up, looking like _____ in a boxing ring.

Exercise III

After studying the roots, prefixes, and suffixes, try to define the following words without using a dictionary.

The prefix *sub* means "under"
The suffix *ize* means "to make"
The root *urb* means "city"

1. suburb: _____._____
2. urbanize: _____
3. substandard: _____
4. standardize: _____

5. subhuman: _____
6. humanize: _____
7. inhuman: _____

8. People leaving cities and moving into the country cause the cities to decay. This is called _____ blight.

7

LESSON THREE

Exercise I ///

In your own words, write a brief definition for as many words on the list as you can. Then correct and/or complete the lesson by using the mini-dictionary in the back of this book.

1. alacrity
2. ambrosia
3. competent
4. complacent
5. conspicuously
6. dapper
7. dejected
8. desolate
9. elation
10. exhilarate
11. grisly
12. incessant
13. prudent
14. scant
15. whimsy

Exercise II //

From the list of words, fill in the blanks to make complete sentences. Some words may have to be changed in form to fit the sentence by using plurals or adding "ed," "ly," "ing," etc.

1. The _____ look on the salesman's face made me want to leave the room.

2. Bread and gravy may seem like _____ to a starving man.

3. Betty, usually lazy, responded with such _____ that her mother was astonished.

4. Mr. Jones indulged every _____ of his only daughter, no matter how odd it seemed.

5. Gene was hired as the new chauffeur since he was a very _____ driver.

6. After his team lost the championship game, Tom was _____ for weeks.

7. After a boring week at work behind a desk, Jack found it _____ to go skydiving on weekends.

8. The car had been abandoned in a(n) _____ area on the edge of the city.

9. My rude cousin gives his mother only_____ respect.

10. Bill was _____ absent from his best friend's bachelor party.

11. We were filled with _____ when our team won the pennant.

12. Basil looked quite _____ in his new uniform.

13. The dog's _____ howling night and day got on everyone's nerves.

14. Be _____ and choose your words wisely, or you may be sorry.

15. It was such a(n) _____ scene that even the policemen were upset.

Exercise III

After studying the roots, prefixes, and suffixes, try to define the following words without using a dictionary.

The prefix *poly* means "many"
The prefix *mono* means "one"
The root *chrom* means "color"
The root *mania* means "an intense enthusiasm; craze"

1. polychromatic: _____
2. monochromatic: _____
3. kleptomania: _____
4. monotonous: _____
5. monorail: _____
6. monomania: _____
7. maniac: _____
8. polygon: _____

LESSON FOUR

Exercise I //

In your own words, write a brief definition for as many words on the list as you can. Then correct and/or complete the lesson by using the mini-dictionary in the back of this book.

1. discern
2. ecstasy
3. eminent
4. exuberant
5. fiscal
6. grotesque
7. hypothetical
8. imperative
9. indignant
10. indolent
11. indubitably
12. inexplicable
13. interpose
14. veer
15. vex

Exercise II //

From the list of words, fill in the blanks to make complete sentences. Some words may have to be changed in form to fit the sentence by using plurals or adding "ed," "ly," "ing," etc.

1. Don't _____ the coach, or he won't let you try out for the team.

2. His _____ spirit was contagious.

3. The car had to _____ sharply to the left to avoid a collision.

4. A look of pure_____ flooded her face when she was crowned Prom Queen.

5. The company's _____ year ended in July.

6. It is _____ that he remains in hiding until the killer is caught.

7. Can you _____ where that noise is coming from?

8. It was a _____ painting, but it drew a huge crowd.

9. His _____ reply was justified after he had been cheated.

10. Ian was _____ the most arrogant person I ever met.

11. Captain Smith could not understand the_____ behavior of the new recruits.

12. It was a shock when the _____ bank president lost his job for bribing a congressman.

13. The scientist wanted to _____a barrier between the liquids.

14. Mark's jobs never lasted more than a week because of his _____ attitude.

15. The science teacher was trying to get her students to understand the difference between a _____ and theoretical situation.

Exercise III ///

After studying the roots, prefixes, and suffixes, try to define the following words without using a dictionary.

   The root *bible* means "book"
   The root *mort* means "death"
   The root *voc, vok,* means "call"

1. bibliography: _____
2. biblical: _____
3. mortician: _____
4. vocation: _____
5. mortuary: _____
6. revoke: _____
7. vocal: _____
8. vocalize: _____
9. When a law is said to be irrevocable, it means _____.

LESSON FIVE

Exercise I //

In your own words, write a brief definition for as many words on the list as can. Then correct and/or complete the lesson by using the mini-dictionary in the back of this book.

1. arduous
2. ascertain
3. awe
4. brevity
5. candid
6. chortle
7. credible
8. eclipse
9. eloquence
10. extinct
11. giddy
12. implore
13. impulse
14. impunity
15. melancholy

Exercise II //

From the list of words, fill in the blanks to make complete sentences. Some words may have to be changed in form to fit the sentence by using plurals or adding "ed," "ly," "ing," etc.

1. The eyewitness gave a(n) _____ account of the robbery.

2. After their _____ journey across the plains, the weary travelers were delighted to see a cool mountain spring.

3. The old ranch hand began to_____ under his breath as he watched the young boy trying to mount the large horse.

4. The policeman was trying to _____ the details of the traffic accident.

5. If you want a(n) _____ opinion of the movie, just ask my father.

6. The _____ of the trial came as a surprise to the news media, which had predicted it would last for months.

7. When the girl saw the baseball star come out of the gate, a look of _____ came over her face.

8. The rainy, gray week did not help her _____ mood.

9. She had bought the red dress on _____ and now hated it.

10. The animals were confused during the solar _____ because they knew it was not yet night time.

11. I must _____ you to reconsider your decision.

12. The eagle was in danger of becoming _____ .

13. The _____ of the child's plea moved the jury to tears.

14. As the parade drew near, the children became _____ with excitement.

15. Because he was police chief, he thought he could do whatever he wished with _____, but the courts set him straight.

Exercise III

Words in Context

No one, not even excellent readers, knows every word in every passage they read; however, the effective reader is able to pick up the meaning of an unfamiliar word from the way the word is used in the passage. Sometimes a definition for a word may be found right in the sentence.

For example:

Although the doctors could not *concur* on the cause, they did *agree* that something had to be done quickly.

From the sentence, we see that *concur* must mean the same thing as *agree*.

At other times, however, while the word is not defined in the sentence, the sense of the sentence tells us what the word must be. In the following sentence, write the word in the blank space that you think belongs there.

No one knew why the boat overturned. There was no storm, there were no waves, and the water was very _____ .

If we rewrite that sentence now, and include the word *placid*, what does this word mean?

No one knew why the boat overturned. There was no storm, there were no waves, and the water was very *placid*.

Keep these two points in mind as you do the next exercise.

Which word in each of the following sentences means about the same thing as the italicized word.

1. The huge bass sped through the water and sucked the bait and hook into its *cavernous* mouth.

   A word that means about the same as *cavernous* is _____.

2. Safety instructions are important for *novices* in sport fishing, for newcomers may be easily injured.

   A word that means about the same as *novices* is_____.

3. All fishermen must be alert when on a boat, for it is only through *vigilance* that accidents are avoided.

   A word that means about the same as *vigilance* is _____.

4. Many *hazards* face new fishermen; one of these dangers is getting stuck with a hook.

   A word that means about the same as *hazards* is_____.

5. *Anglers* often use canoes, for with a canoe, fishermen are able to cover larger areas.
    A word that means about the same as *anglers* is _____.

    Use the information in the following sentences to select a word that is similar in meaning to the italicized word.

6. The bass *lunged* straight out of the water and into the air.
    lunged means: _____
    >   a. ran   b. voiced   c. jumped   d. followed

7. The bass, once only found on the East Coast, has been *transplanted* and may now be found in every state in the country.
    transplanted means: _____
    >   a. moved   b. painted   c. killed   d. opened

8. For your *initial* fishing trip, you should use simple equipment.
    initial means: _____
    >   a. pleasant   b. every   c. first   d. ocean

9. Rod, reel, line, and lures are the basic *components* needed for fishing.
    components means: _____
    >   a. shaped   b. parts   c. only   d. second

10. The *rudimentary* skills of sport fishing should be taught by a skilled fisherman.
    rudimentary means: _____
    >   a. fish   b. water   c. friendly   d. basic

LESSON SIX

Exercise I

In your own words, write a brief definition for as many words on the list as you can. Then correct and/or complete the lesson by using the mini-dictionary in the back of this book.

1.   belated
2.   brogue
3.   condescended
4.   cumulative
5.   dissuade
6.   equitable
7.   fervent
8.   fraternity
9.   gigantic
10. inert
11. infectious
12. interminable
13. invalid
14. terse
15. vague

Exercise II

From the list of words, fill in the blanks to make complete sentences. Some words may have to be changed in form to fit the sentence by using plurals or adding "ed," "ly," "ing," etc.

1.   His _____ comments left plenty of time for questions.

2.   Kathleen's Irish _____ was not as noticeable after two years in the States.

3.   A(n) _____ thank-you card is better than none at all.

4.   When questioned about the robbery, John aroused the policewoman's suspicious because his answers were so _____.

5.   Although he did not wish to talk with me, he _____ to because he wanted to copy my homework.

6.   At the end of the school year, this report will go in your _____ folder.

7. He did not renew it, so now his license is _____ .

8. I sat home waiting for the telephone to ring; the wait seemed _____.

9. Many young freshmen want to join a(n) _____ in college.

10. I had hoped to _____ my brother from taking that job, but he wouldn't listen to me.

11. The car dealer gave us a(n) _____ deal on our purchase; as always, my brother said we were cheated.

12. Her _____ laugh got us all giggling, and we couldn't stop.

13. It was a(n) _____ building with at least fifty floors.

14. The dog was always slow, but he was becoming more tired and nearly _____ as he grew older.

15. The chaplain said a(n) _____ prayer for all those going off to battle.

Exercise III //

After studying the roots, prefixes, and suffixes, try to define the following words without using a dictionary.

The root *term* means "end"
The root *ver* means "true"
The root *tempor* means "time"

1. terminal: _____
2. terminate: _____
3. exterminate: _____
4. temporal: _____
5. temporary: _____
6. contemporary: _____
7. verifiable: _____
8. verify: _____
9. verity: _____
10. Something that is said not to be able to be ended is _____.

LESSON SEVEN

Exercise I ///

In your own words, write a brief definition for as many words on the list as you can. Then correct and/or complete the lesson by using the mini-dictionary in the back of this book.

1. atheist
2. browse
3. collide
4. deformed
5. dwindle
6. frigid
7. ghastly
8. modification
9. obsolete
10. overwhelming
11. plateau
12. reformation
13. rehabilitate
14. renounce
15. sinister

Exercise II ///

From the list of words, fill in the blanks to make complete sentences. Some words may have to be changed in form to fit the sentence by using plurals or adding "ed," "ly," "ing," etc.

1. When we finally reached the second _____, we decided that mountain climbing was for goats.

2. There was a(n) _____ response to the editorial about the mayor.

3. The king decided to _____ his throne in order to marry a commoner.

4. I would rather _____ through a dress shop than actually purchase something.

5. There are federal programs which try to _____ vacant houses and make them livable.

6. Only one _____ was needed to make the race car useable on the street.

7. Soon after the blockade began, the supply of food began to _____ .

8. It looked as if the airplane would _____ with the mountain in a matter of seconds.

9. The mountain air was _____, and every breath was painful.

10. The portable typewriter looked _____ among all the new computers.

11. We were frightened because of the_____ look on his face and the gun in his hand.

12. The church's _____ brought an increase in membership.

13. His left arm was _____ and hung at an odd angle.

14. When Joann said she did not believe in God, her father said she would have to move out because he would not have a(n) _____ in his house.

15. The dead bodies were a(n) _____ reminder of the horrors of war.

Exercise III

Review: Antonyms and Synonyms

For each word list one synonym (means the same), and one antonym (means the opposite).

		Synonym	Antonym
1.	meager	_____	_____
2.	rejection	_____	_____
3.	prudent	_____	_____
4.	grotesque	_____	_____
5.	vex	_____	_____
6.	brevity	_____	_____
7.	implore	_____	_____
8.	melancholy	_____	_____
9.	dissuade	_____	_____
10.	gigantic	_____	_____

LESSON EIGHT

//

In your own words, write a brief definition for as many words on the list as you can. Then correct and/or complete the lesson by using the mini-dictionary in the back of this book.

1.   avid
2.   captive
3.   celebrity
4.   domain
5.   exquisite
6.   hideous
7.   knack
8.   malady
9.   mourn
10.   phantom
11.   predator
12.   prey
13.   texture
14.   valor
15.   woe

Exercise II //

From the list of words, fill in the blanks to make complete sentences. Some words may have to be changed in form to fit the sentence by using plurals or adding "ed," "ly," "ing," etc.

1.   The coarse _____ of the woolen coat scratched her delicate skin.

2.   The diamond jewelry was _____ and very expensive.

3.   He moved like a _____ through the swirling mist.

4.   The hero had shown great _____ and was rewarded by his country.

5.   People_____ the death of Lincoln for years.

6.   _____ will come to anyone who breaks the commandments.

7. It was his _____ for finding lost things that led to his career as a private detective.

8. There was a _____ scar on his face after the car accident.

9. Elka was treated like a(n) _____ when she returned to her small hometown after an appearance on television.

10. The hungry tiger stalked his _____ into the deep jungle.

11. We were held _____ with our own weapons.

12. He was a(n) _____ reader, and during the summer had read 12 novels.

13. The minister said that he suffered not from a physical _____ , but a spiritual one.

14. This is my _____, and you are trespassing.

15. Although some people think of them as an endangered species to be protected, ranchers see wolves as _____ who kill and eat their sheep.

Exercise III

After studying the roots, prefixes, and suffixes, try to define the following words without using a dictionary.

The root *corp* means "body"
The root *rupt* means "break"
The suffix *tion* means "the act of"
The prefix *inter* means "into"

1. interruption _____
2. corruptible _____
3. rupture _____
4. corporal _____
5. corporation _____
6. incorruptible _____
7. interrupt _____
8. erupt _____
9. corrupt _____

LESSON NINE

Exercise I

In your own words, write a brief definition for as many words on the list as you can. Then correct and/or complete the lesson by using the mini-dictionary in the back of this book.

1. amiable
2. deception
3. deflate
4. fissure
5. fraud
6. garment
7. genial
8. ladle
9. loathe
10. mortal
11. rove
12. rural
13. seethe
14. sentimental
15. uncanny

Exercise II

From the list of words, fill in the blanks to make complete sentences. Some words may have to be changed in form to fit the sentence by using plurals or adding "ed," "ly," "ing," etc.

1. The old man had a(n) _____ memory for details.

2. He was guilty of _____ for lying on his tax return.

3. I absolutely _____ dishonest people.

4. Harry was a(n) _____ host as he greeted the new neighbors.

5. The camp counselors were a(n) _____ bunch of teenagers.

6. As all fathers know, men can be just as _____ as women.

7.   I wanted to _____ his oversized ego.

8.   The chef used a silver _____ to serve the soup.

9.   The hungry cattle started to _____ through the cornfields.

10. Her anger began to _____ like a volcano ready to erupt.

11. My aunt works in a(n) _____ factory making uniforms.

12. We moved from the city to a(n) _____ community.

13. The ancient Greeks believed that though men were _____, the gods lived forever.

14. After hiding his saddle in a(n) _____ , the cowboy started walking down the side of the mountain.

15. If you are once caught in an act of _____ , it is hard for anyone to believe in or trust you a second time.

Exercise III //

While analogies can be a bit confusing when first seen, once the logic of the question is understood, analogies can be viewed as challenging mind games. Here is the strategy we recommend to arrive at the best answer.

1.   Change the symbols into words.
     pistol : weapon :: rose : _____
     A **pistol** is to a **weapon** as a **rose** is to a _____ .

2.   Determine the relationship in the first set and put it in a sentence.
     A **pistol** is one kind of a **weapon**.

3.   Complete the second part.
     A **pistol** is one kind of a **weapon**; therefore, a **rose** is one kind of **flower**.
     Analogies can be many different types, but the most common types are the following:
     synonyms – calm : peaceful :: anger : rage
     opposites – praise : criticize :: log cabin : mansion

1. black : white :: abundant : _____
2. audacity : boldness :: fast : _____
3. literate : illiterate :: run : _____
4. no : yes :: praise : _____
5. cold : hot :: ascend : _____
6. mild : harsh :: clement : _____

LESSON TEN

Exercise I //

In your own words, write a brief definition for as many words on the list as you can. Then correct and/or complete the lesson by using the mini-dictionary in the back of this book.

1.   betrayal

2.   edible

3.   eternal

4.   mistreatment

5.   picturesque

6.   pilfer

7.   prompt

8.   refuge

9.   refugee

10. salutation

11. seize

12. stow

13. tarry

14. vile

15. vital

Exercise II //

From the list of words, fill in the blanks to make complete sentences. Some words may have to be changed in form to fit the sentence by using plurals or adding "ed," "ly," "ing," etc.

1.   He hated to see many messages on the answering machine because he believed it should be used only for those which are _____ .

2.   We found _____ from the storm in a cave.

3.   The ASPCA tries to prevent the _____ of animals.

4.   My friend Joe was a _____ from Poland during World War II.

5.   In August 1990, Iraq crossed the border to _____ control of Kuwait.

6.   Most people believe that the human soul is _____ .

24

7. For the _____ of his country, the traitor was executed.

8. The _____ -tasting medicine was hard to swallow.

9. Mom told us not to _____, or we would be late for dinner.

10. The recruits were told to _____ their gear in the small footlockers.

11. The mountain lake was a(n) _____ setting for a canoe ride.

12. As I got off the plane in Hawaii, my first _____ was an orchid lei followed by a kiss.

13. The hamburgers in the diner were barely _____ .

14. He thought that since he only took small amounts of change no one would notice that he had _____ money from the cash register.

15. Our driver was always _____, so we never had to wait for our ride.

Exercise III

After studying the roots, prefixes, and suffixes, try to define the following words without using a dictionary.

The prefixes *il, im, ir* all mean "not"
The prefix *liber* means "free"
The root *soph* means "wisdom"
The root *potent* means "power"
The root *phil* means "love"

1. philosopher: _____
2. sophomore: _____
3. sophist: _____
4. illiberal: _____
5. impotent: _____
6. potentate: _____
7. liberty: _____
8. liberate: _____
9. liberal: _____
10. The mother had wanted to name her baby girl Agnes; the father, hoping the girl would grow to be wise, named her _____.

LESSON ELEVEN

Exercise I //

In your own words, write a brief definition for as many words on the list as you can. Then correct and/or complete the lesson by using the mini-dictionary in the back of this book.

1. chaos
2. courteous
3. decipher
4. gimmick
5. gracious
6. immense
7. infirm
8. punctual
9. ravine
10. reverence
11. sanctity
12. trench
13. unconcern
14. velocity
15. vial

Exercise II //

From the list of words, fill in the blanks to make complete sentences. Some words may have to be changed in form to fit the sentence by using plurals or adding "ed," "ly," "ing," etc.

1. It is not _____ to laugh in someone's face.

2. The house was so _____ that they could go days without seeing each other.

3. She led the guests into the dining room with a(n) _____ smile.

4. John was usually _____, but this time he was late.

5. The soldiers hastily dug a(n) _____ in which to hide.

6. Bill showed his _____ by yawning deeply and looking away.

7. The wind's _____ was increasing, so we all knew it was going to be a bad storm.

8. He cut his finger on a(n) _____ he broke in chemistry lab.

9. If you need a(n) _____ to sell something, you're not a very good salesman.

10. It was difficult to _____ the note he had written.

11. The colt was trapped in a(n) _____ which was overgrown with weeds.

12. In the _____ that followed the earthquake, many children were separated from their families.

13. Most people believe in the _____ of marriage.

14. The minister's voice was filled with _____ as he led the prayer service.

15. My grandfather, who was _____ for many years, spent his last days in a nursing home.

Exercise III //

After studying the roots, prefixes, and suffixes, try to define the following words without using a dictionary.

The root *phon* means "sound"
The prefix *tele* means "distance"
The suffix *ic* means "of, or having the characteristic of"
The root *path* means "feeling"

1. telephone: _____
2. television: _____
3. polyphonic: _____
4. telepathic: _____
5. telegraph: _____
6. telepathy: _____
7. phonics: _____

LESSON TWELVE

Exercise I

In your own words, write a brief definition for as many words on the list as you can. Then correct and/or complete the lesson by using the mini-dictionary in the back of this book.

1. brutality
2. current
3. dismiss
4. fortunate
5. intimate
6. paralysis
7. revert
8. sanctuary
9. solicit
10. spectacle
11. substantiate
12. tamper
13. topical
14. wharf
15. whine

Exercise II

From the list of words, fill in the blanks to make complete sentences. Some words may have to be changed in form to fit the sentence by using plurals or adding "ed," "ly," "ing," etc.

1. Drug companies have made their packages _____ -proof.

2. Charitable organizations sometimes _____ money over the telephone.

3. There was no one who could _____ his alibi.

4. Temporary _____ is often caused by a pinched nerve.

5. The display of fireworks was a _____ we all enjoyed.

6. When it rains in the city, you are _____ if you can locate a taxi quickly.

28

7. They told him his driver's license was expired and he needed a(n) _____ one before he could get insurance.

8. The busy _____ was crowded with workers unloading the big ships.

9. The refugees found _____ in a new land.

10. A minor burn usually needs a(n) _____ medication.

11. The puppy began to _____ when he was taken from his mother.

12. If Mary remarried, her inheritance would _____ to her late husband's estate.

13. Because of the heavy snowfall, we were _____ early from school.

14. Because of the man's _____ toward the dogs, the ASPCA had him arrested.

15. We were _____ friends and shared many secrets.

Exercise III //

Words In Context

An earlier exercise in lesson five was rather easy because there was only one target word, but with two or more unfamiliar words it could become more difficult. Try the next exercise. If you run into a problem, you may look up the meaning of **one** *of the words in a dictionary.*

For each italicized word write a brief definition.

1. The bank manager *absconded* with more than one million dollars of the bank's money, but Scotland Yard caught him, and he was *extradited* to the United States.
   absconded - _____
   extradited - _____

2. Even though the man expected to spend the rest of his life *languishing* in jail, he was able to escape because of the *laxity* of his jailers.
   languishing - _____
   laxity - _____

3. The governor found the warden and two guards *culpable* in the escape; he *terminated* their services, and they are now drawing unemployment benefits.
   culpable - _____
   terminated - _____

29

LESSON THIRTEEN

Exercise I ///

In your own words, write a brief definition for as many words on the list as you can. Then correct and/or complete the lesson by using the mini-dictionary in the back of this book.

1.   abduct
2.   brusque
3.   contradict
4.   emulate
5.   feign
6.   flank
7.   fragile
8.   hereditary
9.   limber
10. plague
11. reign
12. sensible
13. spasm
14. taunt
15. tempest

Exercise II ///

From the list of words, fill in the blanks to make complete sentences. Some words may have to be changed in form to fit the sentence by using plurals or adding "ed," "ly," "ing," etc.

1.   My legs aren't as _____ as they were in my younger days.

2.   Blue eyes and blonde hair are factors caused by _____ .

3.   His _____ manner made people avoid him.

4.   The older children began to _____ the smaller child and made him cry.

5.   If you _____ everything he says, he will stop saying anything at all to you.

6.   In order to stay home from school, he _____ an illness.

7. Brutus sent horsemen to attack Caesar's right _____.

8. The _____ teacup had been made years ago and was worn thin by use.

9. The family knew someone had to have _____ the dog, as he never would have left the yard on his own.

10. It was a _____ plan to travel at night to avoid the heat of the day.

11. After the accident I had a muscle _____ in my right shoulder.

12. Children often try to _____ their heroes.

13. Hitler's _____ of terror brought death to millions.

14. The storm was a _____ that would not be soon forgotten.

15. The Black Death was a _____ that swept across Europe during the Middle Ages.

Exercise III

For each word list one synonym and one antonym.

		Synonym	Antonym
1.	ghastly	_____	_____
2.	sinister	_____	_____
3.	mourn	_____	_____
4.	valor	_____	_____
5.	amiable	_____	_____
6.	deflate	_____	_____
7.	genial	_____	_____
8.	rural	_____	_____
9.	prompt	_____	_____
10.	internal	_____	_____

LESSON FOURTEEN

Exercise I //

In your own words, write a brief definition for as many words on the list as you can. Then correct and/or complete the lesson by using the mini-dictionary in the back of this book.

1. bewitch
2. emerge
3. eviction
4. humiliate
5. jeopardy
6. luminous
7. mansion
8. mirage
9. modest
10. oblivious
11. prominent
12. ramble
13. sludge
14. varmint
15. vindictive

Exercise II //

From the list of words, fill in the blanks to make complete sentences. Some words may have to be changed in form to fit the sentence by using plurals or adding "ed," "ly," "ing," etc.

1. The governor's _____ was open to the public during the holiday season.

2. I'm not usually a(n) _____ person unless I've been treated badly by someone.

3. Scarlett O'Hara tried to _____ Rhett Butler with her charms.

4. The candles in the window were _____ as they glowed in the darkness.

5. Mr. Bailey was a(n) _____ attorney who had won many difficult cases.

6. Suddenly the bow of the Russian submarine _____ from the dark waters.

7.   Seeing a(n) _____ in the desert is not an uncommon occurrence.

8.   _____ notices were sent to three families in the apartment house who were behind in their rent.

9.   Martha felt _____ by the drug conviction of her brother.

10. The _____ little house was comfortable, even though it lacked modern conveniences.

11. The girl was _____ to everything as she stared blankly into the dark shadows.

12. The success of the mission was in _____ because of one man's carelessness.

13. The beach was covered with _____ from the last oil spill.

14. His speech began to _____ as he got older and more feeble.

15. When Mr. Baxter said that he had shot at a _____ that tried to steal some eggs from his henhouse, I knew that he was talking about my pet raccoon.

Exercise III //

Here are some more types of analogies. Notice the first one is not an antonym and not exactly a synonym. Rather, "warm" and "hot" are different in degree in the same way "smile" is like, but less than, "laugh."

degree – warm : hot :: smile : laugh

In this second type, the relationship is person to object. An engineer operates a train as a pilot operates an airplane.

person to object – engineer : train :: pilot : airplane

In the third kind of analogy, the relationship is that of function. A car goes in a garage as an airplane goes in a hangar.

function – car : garage :: airplane : hangar

1.   trot : run :: _____ : thrash

2.   teacher : classroom :: judge : _____

3.   train : terminal :: boat: _____

LESSON FIFTEEN

Exercise I //

In your own words, write a brief definition for as many words on the list as you can. Then correct and/or complete the lesson by using the mini-dictionary in the back of this book.

1. ancestor
2. animosity
3. beneficial
4. compress
5. concise
6. drudgery
7. dubious
8. elapse
9. gorgeous
10. initiate
11. pauper
12. precise
13. ruin
14. strenuous
15. tinge

Exercise II //

From the list of words, fill in the blanks to make complete sentences. Some words may have to be changed in form to fit the sentence by using plurals or adding "ed," "ly," "ing," etc.

1. Her lips _____ in anger as the excuse got more unbelievable.

2. Jogging can be a _____ exercise if you're not in good physical condition.

3. Jury selection had been difficult, and the lawyer was now _____ about the outcome of her case.

4. In cooking, many people use a pinch of salt or a dash of pepper because _____ measurements are not important.

5. The sergeant's _____ instructions wasted no words.

34

6. The counselor told him that he had to deal with the _____ he felt toward authority figures.

7. A high school diploma is helpful in receiving a good job, but a college degree is even more _____.

8. They both wanted to talk to each other, but neither knew how to _____ a conversation.

9. I felt like a _____ when I discovered I had only $1.50 to my name.

10. If you let too much time _____, you could lose the race.

11. His skin had a yellowish _____ as if he were jaundiced.

12. The _____ sunset was breathtaking to see.

13. The storm did not _____ the house, but the tourists who came later did.

14. My _____ came from Ireland, but I was born in America.

15. Cleaning stables was pure _____, but the pay was not bad.

Exercise III

After studying the roots, prefixes, and suffixes, try to define the following words without using a dictionary.

The root *ped, pod* refers to "foot"
The root *phob* means "fear"
The root *scop* means "watch"
The root *port* means "to carry, bring"
The prefix *bi* means "two"

   A. A creature with two legs is called a _____ , but a stand with three legs is call a _____ .
   B. If you had a fear of enclosed places you are suffering from_____ia, while a bibliophobe would fear _____.
   C. Give a literal meaning for these words.
       1. report   _____
       2. transport   _____
       3. portable   _____
       4. import   _____
       5. porter   _____

35

LESSON SIXTEEN

Exercise I //

In your own words, write a brief definition for as many words on the list as you can. Then correct and/or complete the lesson by using the mini-dictionary in the back of this book.

1. bulge
2. engulf
3. envious
4. evolution
5. expunge
6. frail
7. implication
8. intensive
9. nimble
10. nutrition
11. obliterate
12. pamper
13. taint
14. ventilate
15. waver

Exercise II //

From the list of words, fill in the blanks to make complete sentences. Some words may have to be changed in form to fit the sentence by using plurals or adding "ed," "ly," "ing," etc.

1. The theory of _____ teaches that man came from apes.

2. The speech did not state that the opposition was lying, but the _____ was there.

3. Exercise and proper _____ are essential for good health.

4. Even though she looked _____, the old woman was able to control the prancing horse with just a touch.

5. Uncle Bill is not as _____ as he was in his younger days.

6. I wanted to _____ the unpleasant memories from my mind.

7. We tried to _____ the stuffy room with the overhead fans.

8. The slight _____ in his coat pocket could have been a pistol.

9. Mrs. McGee liked to _____ her grandchildren.

10. She was _____ of her best friend's sudden wealth.

11. Her love began to _____ between her father and her handcuffed boyfriend.

12. After an _____ search on the grounds, we found the missing jewelry.

13. A small group of U.S. Marines were almost _____ by a very large enemy force.

14. His mother said that one good deed would not _____ all the past evil acts he had committed.

15. As the old saying goes, one bad person can _____ the reputation of a whole group.

Exercise III

After studying the roots, prefixes, and suffixes, try to define the following words without using a dictionary.

The root *tract* means "to draw"
The root *ven, vent* means "to come"
The root *anthro* means "man"
The suffix *ology* means "the study of"
The prefix *com, con* means "together with"

A. The study of man must be _____, but one who hates mankind is a mis _____ while a creature that resembles man is called an _____ poid.

B. List other words you can think of that end in *ology* and, as well as you can, identify what the word is a study of.

C. Give the literal meaning of these words:
   1. convention   _____
   2. prevention   _____
   3. invention   _____

37

LESSON SEVENTEEN

Exercise I

In your own words, write a brief definition for as many words on the list as you can. Then correct and/or complete the lesson by using the mini-dictionary in the back of this book.

1.   annex
2.   belligerent
3.   crest
4.   cubicle
5.   dilemma
6.   encore
7.   lament
8.   mingle
9.   monotony
10. mural
11. raucous
12. scorch
13. solemn
14. vengeance
15. wary

Exercise II

From the list of words, fill in the blanks to make complete sentences. Some words may have to be changed in form to fit the sentence by using plurals or adding "ed," "ly," "ing," etc.

1.   The new _____ on the courthouse wall was a welcome improvement.

2.   She faced quite a _____, because she didn't want to hurt anyone's feelings.

3.   The small boat hurtled along on the _____ of the enormous wave.

4.   The young boy who saw his parents shot vowed he would get _____ on the invaders.

5.   We could hear _____ laughter coming from the back of the saloon.

6. After his second _____, the pianist bowed and left the stage.

7. The twelve-year-old bully always had a(n) _____ look on his face.

8. The thief tried to _____ with the commuters at the bus terminal, but the police soon found him.

9. The witnesses were being held in a(n) _____ next to the courtroom.

10. With a(n) _____ look in both directions, the young girl crossed the street.

11. The _____ of the speeches put many people to sleep.

12. In a(n) _____ voice, the minister began the morning service.

13. The children put their coats and hats in a(n) _____ built into the back of the room.

14. He was a true friend, and I do greatly _____ his leaving.

15. If you put that hot iron on my jacket, you will _____ it.

Exercise III

For each, list one synonym and one antonym.

		Synonym	Antonym
1.	chaos	_____	_____
2.	gracious	_____	_____
3.	punctual	_____	_____
4.	sanctity	_____	_____
5.	fortunate	_____	_____
6.	solicit	_____	_____
7.	brusque	_____	_____
8.	fragile	_____	_____
9.	precise	_____	_____

LESSON EIGHTEEN

Exercise I

In your own words, write a brief definition for as many words on the list as you can. Then correct and/or complete the lesson by using the mini-dictionary in the back of this book.

1.   astrology
2.   astronomy
3.   beckon
4.   cantankerous
5.   compose
6.   disaster
7.   flurry
8.   grudge
9.   impeccable
10. seldom
11. skeptic
12. squirm
13. treacherous
14. wander
15. zestful

Exercise II

From the list of words, fill in the blanks to make complete sentences. Some words may have to be changed in form to fit the sentence by using plurals or adding "ed," "ly," "ing," etc.

1.   With a small wave, the cashier _____ for the next customer to approach.

2.   She tried to _____ her thoughts before the interview began.

3.   He was such a(n) _____ that he questioned everything that he was told.

4.   He held a(n) _____ against his father for ten years.

5.   The young man had _____ manners except when he chewed his food.

6.   No matter where he _____ , he always comes home for the holidays.

7. It was a(n) _____ meal filled with exciting flavors.

8. There was a _____ of activity when the manager entered the office.

9. It would be a _____ if another hurricane hit the Carolinas so soon after the last one.

10. After twenty minutes, the baby began to _____ off his mother's lap.

11. Mr. Walker is a _____ old shopkeeper who yells at everybody.

12. We carefully walked along a _____ path filled with sharp rocks and branches, but it was the only way to the top.

13. _____ does anything cheerful appear on the news.

14. While many people do believe in _____ , I do not believe that anyone can predict future events this way.

15. The science of _____ truly began when scientists figured out that the Earth circled the sun and not vice versa.

Exercise III

These analogies are of mixed types. See if you can figure out the word needed.

1. Siamese : cat :: mansion : _____
2. go in : come out :: submerge : _____
3. practical : impractical :: modest: _____
4. concise : brief :: dubious : _____
5. rejoice : wedding :: _____ : funeral
6. peak : mountain :: crest : _____

LESSON NINETEEN

Exercise I //

In your own words, write a brief definition for as many words on the list as you can. Then correct and/or complete the lesson by using the mini-dictionary in the back of this book.

1. boorish
2. idiosyncrasy
3. jeer
4. malice
5. marital
6. oppressive
7. pandemonium
8. pensive
9. placate
10. quirk
11. reckon
12. resolute
13. succulent
14. transit
15. urban

Exercise II //

From the list of words, fill in the blanks to make complete sentences. Some words may have to be changed in form to fit the sentence by using plurals or adding "ed," "ly," "ing," etc.

1. Don't try to _____ me; your crude words made me angry.

2. The grapes were so _____ they practically burst open before they were picked.

3. There was a _____ tone in the captain's voice that calmed the rookies and made them feel he was certainly in control.

4. The crowd began to _____ when the bullfighter jumped behind the fence.

5. The air in the crowded room was so _____ that Jack felt he could cut it with a knife.

6. The juror voted guilty because he thought he could see _____ in the eyes of the accused killer.

7. After the game, _____ broke out in the winner's locker room.

8. It was a strange _____ of fate that brought them both to the corner at that exact time.

9. She was in a _____ mood as she remembered the years right after the war.

10. Although everyone may have his or her own _____ , it is hard for people to accept someone else's.

11. The unschooled man_____that the answer to the math problem was $8.00, but he was not certain.

12. I said that he never sent me a letter, but he swore that he did and it must have been lost in _____ .

13. Because of _____ problems, the couple saw a marriage counselor to help save the relationship.

14. He was such a _____ person, that he talked while he ate and the food fell out of his mouth.

15. _____ life offers more opportunities than life in the country, but there are also more dangers.

Exercise III

After studying the roots, prefixes, and suffixes, try to define the following words without using a dictionary.

The root *multi* means "many"
The root *nav, nau* refers to "ships, sailors or the sea"
The root *nov* means "new"
The root *pater, patri* refers to "father"

1. multicolored: _____
2. multitude: _____
3. multiple: _____
4. navigate: _____
5. nautical: _____
6. novice: _____
7. novel: _____
8. paternal: _____
9. paternity: _____

LESSON TWENTY

Exercise I //

In your own words, write a brief definition for as many words on the list as you can. Then correct and/or complete the lesson by using the mini-dictionary in the back of this book.

1. affirm
2. capitulate
3. divert
4. embellish
5. gesticulate
6. indulgent
7. laceration
8. martial
9. navigation
10. ominous
11. quarry
12. sinewy
13. subtle
14. sullen
15. transcend

Exercise II //

From the list of words, fill in the blanks to make complete sentences. Some words may have to be changed in form to fit the sentence by using plurals or adding "ed," "ly," "ing," etc.

1. The sky looked _____ as black clouds covered the sun.

2. The girl's anger showed and gave her a(n) _____ appearance.

3. Falling on the sharp rocks caused an ugly _____ on his shoulder.

4. We tried to _____ the children's attention by showing them pictures in a book.

5. My father likes to _____ his stories with jokes.

6. I can neither _____ nor deny what she told you because I was not there.

7. He gave the crowd such a _____ wink before he left the room that few people saw it.

8. Rather than_____, we will hold our ground; then we will counterattack.

9. The stranded people began to _____ wildly, trying to get the attention of the approaching plane.

10. The_____ attitude of the belligerent country struck fear in the hearts of all their neighbors.

11. You rarely see a talkative, overweight cowboy hero; they are all tight-lipped and_____.

12. While his usual _____ was deer, today he was hunting something far more dangerous.

13. To cross the ocean in a small boat, you need to know a great deal about _____.

14. When you are in competition with yourself, you always try to _____ your last effort.

15. While my father was very strict, his father was so _____ that he let him do anything he wanted.

Exercise III //

After studying the roots, prefixes, and suffixes, try to define the following words without using a dictionary.

The root *scrib, script* means "to write"
The root *stru, struct* means "to build"
The root *tempor* means "time"
The root *therm* means "heat"

A. A thermometer measures _____, but if we want something hot to stay hot, or something cold to stay cold, we would put either of them in a _____. The word which means "pertaining to heat" is _____al.

B. List as many words as you can think of that contain the root "stru," "struct."

C. A conscript is one whose name is _____. A prescription is _____; a description is _____.

45

LESSON TWENTY-ONE

Exercise I

In your own words, write a brief definition for as many words on the list as you can. Then correct and/or complete the lesson by using the mini-dictionary in the back of this book.

1. caress
2. impious
3. intangible
4. malignant
5. miscreant
6. mock
7. nonchalant
8. odor
9. pestilence
10. pious
11. ruminate
12. scrutiny
13. supposition
14. trifle
15. vehemently

Exercise II

From the list of words, fill in the blanks to make complete sentences. Some words may have to be changed in form to fit the sentence by using plurals or adding "ed," "ly," "ing," etc.

1. It was difficult to identify the _____ which was causing the plague.

2. Defacing a church door is a(n) _____ act.

3. I knew I had nothing to be nervous about, even though my tax returns were under _____ by the IRS.

4. Mary thought that his deodorant gave off a worse _____ than the smell it was meant to cover.

5. It is cruel to _____ someone because of the way he or she speaks.

6. He was very excited about the job interview, but when he walked into the office, he tried to appear _____.

7. The sun's harmful rays can cause _____ spots on the skin.

8. The judge _____ pounded his gavel to restore order to the unruly proceeding.

9. The members did not want this _____ in their club because he caused a great deal of trouble.

10. She acted _____ in church but was a wild person when she left.

11. When the wealthy man gave the beggar the money, it was just a(n) _____ to him but a meal to the beggar.

12. I love to go out to the country to _____ on the nature of things and the meaning of life.

13. Jim didn't see anything dangerous, but there was a(n) _____ feel about the old house which was frightening.

14. After a quick _____ she tucked the blankets lovingly around the baby.

15. The prosecution's case was based entirely on _____, not fact.

Exercise III ///

After studying the roots, prefixes and suffixes, try to define the following words without using a dictionary.

The root *am* means "friend, love"
The root *aqu* means "water"
The root *brev* means "short"
The root *mater, matri* means "mother"

1. maternal: _____
2. maternity: _____
3. brevity: _____
4. amity: _____
5. amiable: _____
6. amicable: _____

7. aquarium: _____
8. aquanaut: _____
9. aquaplane: _____
10. aquatic: _____
11. aqueduct: _____
12. aquacade: _____

LESSON TWENTY-TWO

Exercise I ///

In your own words, write a brief definition for as many words on the list as you can. Then correct and/or complete the lesson by using the mini-dictionary in the back of this book.

1. antagonist
2. clique
3. cosmopolitan
4. deprivation
5. graphic
6. indomitable
7. lethargic
8. migrate
9. opaque
10. palatial
11. peonage
12. pliable
13. predominate
14. sly
15. tenacious

Exercise II ///

From the list of words, fill in the blanks to make complete sentences. Some words may have to be changed in form to fit the sentence by using plurals or adding "ed," "ly," "ing," etc.

1. The newspaper gave such a(n) _____ account of the murder that some readers were shocked.

2. In a play it is necessary to have a hero and an _____.

3. If Bret wanted to win this game of espionage, he was going to have to be as _____ as his opponent.

4. Fortunately, the system of _____ has passed out of usage, and a man can pay off his debts in other ways.

5. The hot sun and warm breeze made me feel lazy and _____.

48

6. We saw the effects of the _____ of food upon the starving children.

7. Because of the nature of the game, tall people _____ in basketball.

8. Because the bathroom window was _____, no one could see in; despite that, there was plenty of light in the room.

9. The new shopping mall seemed _____ with crystal chandeliers and fountains.

10. Marcia tried to twist the wire around the pole, but the wire was not _____ enough.

11. As winter approached, the geese began to _____ to a warmer climate.

12. The _____ spirit of Neslon Mandela enabled the oppressed in South Africa to continue the fight against apartheid.

13. The dog held on to the bag with such a _____ grasp that we couldn't get it from him no matter how hard we tried.

14. After touring Europe for a year, Jason seemed very _____ in his attitude toward food.

15. Even Jane, who seemed to enjoy being a rebel, wanted to belong to the _____ in school that was so popular.

Exercise III

After studying the roots, prefixes, and suffixes, try to define the following words without using a dictionary.

The suffix *ism* means "belief in" or "practice of"
The root *cent* refers to "one hundred"
The root *dec* refers to "ten"
The root *duc, duct* means "to lead"
The prefix *anti* means "against"

A. An antidote is _____; guns that shoot at planes are called _____ guns.

B. List as many words as you can think of that contain the root *cent*.

C. A ten year period is called a _____, and a word that originally meant to kill every tenth person is _____ .

D. List as many words as you can think of that contain the root *duc, duct*.

49

LESSON TWENTY-THREE

Exercise I //

In your own words, write a brief definition for as many words on the list as you can. Then correct and/or complete the lesson by using the mini-dictionary in the back of this book.

1.   malleable

2.   naive

3.   obscure

4.   pacify

5.   panacea

6.   plausible

7.   ponder

8.   prosperous

9.   refute

10. ridicule

11. sarcasm

12. serene

13. tedious

14. teeter

15. unanimous

Exercise II //

From the list of words, fill in the blanks to make complete sentences. Some words may have to be changed in form to fit the sentence by using plurals or adding "ed," "ly," "ing," etc.

1.   He gave his mother a(n) _____ excuse for being late for dinner, but she still didn't believe him.

2.   You should not _____ someone for being different.

3.   The defense attorney tried to _____ the testimony of the policeman.

4.   The first time he bought stock, he was _____ enough to think he would make a fortune.

5.   Although poor as a young man, his hard work and intelligence made him very _____ before the age of forty.

6. We all held our breath as the drunken man _____ on the roof.

7. The jury had to _____ all aspects of the trial before they could reach a decision.

8. We could not _____ the screaming child no matter what we did.

9. The _____ in his voice made Joan very angry.

10. Until the war began, Kuwait had been an _____ dot on the map for most Americans.

11. Her face had the _____ quality of a woman at complete peace.

12. My grandmother thinks chicken soup is a _____ for whatever ails you.

13. It was a long and _____ journey without anything to look at or to do.

14. The club members gave their _____ approval of the president's plan.

15. A child's mind and personality are most _____ in the first few years.

Exercise III //

For each word list one synonym and one antonym.

		Synonym	Antonym
1.	seldom	_____	_____
2.	skeptical	_____	_____
3.	placate	_____	_____
4.	resolute	_____	_____
5.	affirm	_____	_____
6.	embellish	_____	_____
7.	pious	_____	_____
8.	opaque	_____	_____
9.	pliable	_____	_____
10.	sly	_____	_____

LESSON TWENTY-FOUR

Exercise I ///

In your own words, write a brief definition for as many words on the list as you can. Then correct and/or complete the lesson by using the mini-dictionary in the back of this book.

1. catapult

2. chateau

3. cliff

4. eccentric

5. fathom

6. introspective

7. lean

8. mythical

9. pertain

10. progeny

11. providence

12. respite

13. slender

14. tranquil

15. transition

Exercise II ///

From the list of words, fill in the blanks to make complete sentences. Some words may have to be changed in form to fit the sentence by using plurals or adding "ed," "ly," "ing," etc.

1. Jill could spend hours in _____ thinking while Jack had to constantly be doing mindless physical activity.

2. The ski lodge was built to look like a French _____ .

3. The most successful models are tall and _____.

4. The car stopped so dangerously close to the edge of the _____ that we were almost afraid to breathe.

5. It was by the_____ of God that the new troops arrived in time to save the day.

6. To prepare the citizens for the _____ from a monarchy to a democracy, the radio station made announcements once every hour.

7. It was his _____ behavior which made the police suspicious of him.

8. The sudden shower gave a short _____ from the hot, humid weather.

9. To be perfectly fair, you must not _____ towards one team or another if you are a referee.

10. I need a (n)_____ setting if I am to write this book because I cannot think in here with all this noise.

11. It was hard to _____ the ever-changing attitude of her friend.

12. His remarks did not _____ to the subject we were discussing.

13. The attackers used a _____ to hurl rocks and burning oil at the castle.

14. In tracing a family tree, it is important to know all the _____ of your ancestors.

15. A unicorn is a _____ creature.

Exercise III //

After studying the roots, prefixes, and suffixes, try to define the following words without using a dictionary.

The root *fort* means "strong"
The root *gen* means "race, kind, birth"
The root *graph* means "to write"
The prefix *mono* means "one"

1. fortress : _____
2. fortitude: _____
3. genre: _____
4. genocide: _____
5. genealogy: _____
6. monograph: _____
7. monotheism: _____
8. monologue: _____

LESSON TWENTY-FIVE

Exercise I //

In your own words, write a brief definition for as many words on the list as you can. Then correct and/or complete the lesson by using the mini-dictionary in the back of this book.

1. colleague
2. degeneration
3. desecrate
4. epilogue
5. equilibrium
6. galley
7. heritage
8. hierarchy
9. interim
10. massive
11. oblique
12. odyssey
13. saga
14. suave
15. subterfuge

Exercise II //

From the list of words, fill in the blanks to make complete sentences. Some words may have to be changed in form to fit the sentence by using plurals or adding "ed," "ly," "ing," etc.

1. Although her name was difficult for most people to say, she would not change it because she was proud of her _____.

2. During the storm, all of the dishes fell from the table in the ship's _____.

3. He gave only _____ answers, never direct ones.

4. Until Tom could return to the job, a(n) _____ president was appointed to take over.

5. The rate of _____ of the cells gave the scientist the clues he needed.

6. The heroic deeds he accomplished made for a(n) _____ that was very exciting to read.

7. They were charged with _____ the graveyard because they had knocked down the headstones.

8. I'm going to the gym to stay in shape, not to develop _____ muscles.

9. It was only through _____ that the troops were able to move secretly into the town.

10. Jim, who works in the art department, is a(n) _____ of Joe, who works in the print shop.

11. It is important to keep your _____ if you are a gymnast.

12. Laura couldn't help but fall in love with the _____ and handsome duke.

13. Jane could never learn the _____ of the British money system.

14. The three-week boat trip turned into a(n) _____ of over six months.

15. It wasn't until we got to the _____ of the play that I really understood what was happening.

Exercise III //

After studying the roots, prefixes, and suffixes, try to define the following words without using a dictionary.

The prefix *ambi, amphi* means "both"
The prefix *super* means "above, beyond"
The root *luc, lum* means "light"

1. amphibian: _____

2. amphibious vehicle: _____

3. ambidextrous : _____

4. supernatural: _____

5. superhuman: _____

6. luminous: _____

7. elucidate: _____

8. illuminate: _____

LESSON TWENTY-SIX

Exercise I //

In your own words, write a brief definition for as many words on the list as you can. Then correct and/or complete the lesson by using the mini-dictionary in the back of this book.

1. abductor
2. accord
3. automaton
4. brazen
5. cardinal
6. chastise
7. contrite
8. facade
9. fiasco
10. frugal
11. Hades
12. mute
13. purgatory
14. ricochet
15. superfluous

Exercise II //

From the list of words, fill in the blanks to make complete sentences. Some words may have to be changed in form to fit the sentence by using plurals or adding "ed," "ly," "ing," etc.

1. John expected his father to_____ him for forgetting to take out the garbage.

2. His clothing and over-bleached hair gave him a hard, _____ look.

3. My first dinner party turned into a(n) _____ when the oven exploded.

4. The waiter moved like a(n) _____ as he served the meal like a robot.

5. I may not look it, but I am very _____ and I will never do it again.

6. Some people think that _____ is a place where you wait until you go to heaven.

7. Father felt that nuts on top of the whipped cream were_____ .

8. The boy remained _____, refusing to say a word.

9. A _____ rule is to treat others kindly.

10. Sometimes the renovation of the downtown area amounts only to applying a _____ to the old buildings.

11. It was so hot in the desert he felt he was in _____ .

12. "Waste not, want not," my _____ grandfather always said.

13. The labor negotiators met with management to see if they could finally reach a(n) _____ to end the strike.

14. The hunter was a poor shot, but the deer was taken down by a shot that _____ off a tree.

15. The _____ demanded $10,000 in ransom.

Exercise III ///

After studying the roots, prefixes, and suffixes, try to define the following words without using a dictionary.

The suffix *ous* means "full of"
The root *magna* means "great, large"
The word element *meter* means "measure"
The root *micro* means "small"

1. magnanimous: _____

2. magnitude: _____

3. magnificent: _____

4. magnify: _____

5. speedometer: _____

6. thermometer: _____

7. microbe: _____

8. microchip: _____

9. microscope: _____

LESSON TWENTY-SEVEN

Exercise I //

In your own words, write a brief definition for as many words on the list as you can. Then correct and/or complete the lesson by using the mini-dictionary in the back of this book.

1.   amateur

2.   comely

3.   demeanor

4.   exhort

5.   fluent

6.   gaunt

7.   grovel

8.   homely

9.   impose

10.   inarticulate

11.   metamorphose

12.   predestination

13.   reminiscence

14.   sage

15.   sedative

Exercise II //

From the list of words, fill in the blanks to make complete sentences. Some words may have to be changed in form to fit the sentence by using plurals or adding "ed," "ly," "ing," etc.

1.   The _____ of a caterpillar into a butterfly is something to behold.

2.   Even though she was born abroad, Zet's English was _____, without a trace of an accent.

3.   His _____ never changed, but inside he was angry.

4.   Cheerleaders _____ the crowd to cheer and the team to win.

5.   He was very shy and _____, but we knew that with a lot of practice he could become a good speaker.

58

6. As a young girl she was _____, but when she matured, she became beautiful.

7. Listening to his _____ was like reading a history book.

8. I hated to humble myself, but I made myself _____ to get my job back.

9. Sue hated to _____ on their hospitality, but she did not want to leave during the storm.

10. The learned professor was often sought out for his _____ comments.

11. The tall, blonde model was very _____, but she had no personality.

12. The doctor gave me a _____ to help me sleep.

13. If you accept money for a performance, you may lose your _____ status.

14. Some people believe in _____, but I don't believe God has a plan for us.

15. After two weeks in the jungle, his face had become _____ .

Exercise III

Read the paragraph and choose the word or words that best defines the target word.

1. When asked to decide whether or not he supported the bill, the senator could not make up his mind. He *vacillated* between opposing the new tax and supporting it. In fact, he changed his mind three times.

    A. support   B. strengthen   C. go back and forth   D. weaken

2. The human body needs food and water in order to *sustain* life. After a few days without eating, a person would grow extremely weak and eventually would die.

    A. support   B. remove   C. hang   D. drag

3. "You have no *scruples*!" he shouted. "You are my brother and I love you, but I do not like the things you do. You lie, you cheat, and you steal. You will do anything to get ahead for yourself, no matter how much it hurts someone else."

    A. fear   B. conscience   C. rights   D. sadness

LESSON TWENTY-EIGHT

Exercise I ///

In your own words, write a brief definition for as many words on this list as you can. Then correct and/or complete the lesson by using the mini-dictionary in the back of this book.

1. assert
2. collaborator
3. covet
4. depreciate
5. dialogue
6. flout
7. inconsequential
8. intoxication
9. monologue
10. peer
11. scrutinize
12. stupor
13. torpor
14. transplant
15. vivacity

Exercise II ///

From the list of words, fill in the blanks to make complete sentences. Some words may have to be changed in form to fit the sentence by using plurals or adding "ed," "ly," "ing," etc.

1. A type of_____ can come from winning, as well as from drinking.

2. There is no reason to _____ the rules just because you don't agree with them.

3. Wanda wanted a _____ on the project, but no one volunteered to help.

4. One should not _____ another man's wife or home or money.

5. The drug caused such a _____ -like state he could barely remember his own name.

6. The best time to _____ a tree is in the spring.

7.   We expect to be tried by a jury of our _____ .

8.   "We will never finish with this project if you _____ every little detail," Wanda said to Tim.

9.   "I thought we were going to have a conversation, not a _____," the mother said to her son after listening to him for five minutes.

10. "I want to see as much _____ as possible," the cheerleader's coach said at tryouts.

11. "The _____ is too odd in the first act," the director said to the actors.

12. "Nothing is _____ in science," said the professor.

13. I couldn't believe it when the salesman told me that my new car would _____ by one thousand dollars as soon as I drove off the lot.

14. After lunch, staying awake is hard because of the _____ I feel.

15. All the man wanted to do was _____ his rights under the constitution, but no one would let him talk.

Exercise III

These analogies are of mixed types. See if you can figure out the type of relationship needed.

1.   oppress : keep down :: ponder: _____
2.   pious : impious :: rural : _____
3.   ridicule: praise :: arouse : _____
4.   placid : agitated :: innocent : _____
5.   hovel : hut :: chateau : _____
6.   beginning : end :: prologue : _____
7.   fool : foolish :: _____ : sagacious
8.   appreciate : depreciate :: _____ : professional

Mini - Dictionary

Mini - Dictionary

abduct   (ăb dŭkt´)   to kidnap

abductor   (ăb dŭk´ tər)   kidnapper

accessible   (ăk sĕs´ ə bəl)   easy to reach

accord   (ə kôrd´)   mutual agreement; harmony

acute   (ə kyōōt´)   severe and sharp; keen

adamant   (ăd´ ə mənt)   unyielding; firm; stubborn

affirm   (ə fûrm´)   to state positively; assert to be true

alacrity   (ə lăk´ rĭ tē)   quick willingness; eager readiness

amateur   (ăm´ ə chōōr)   not a professional

ambrosia   (ăm brō´ zhə)   anything that tastes or smells delicious

amiable   (ā´ mē ə bəl)   good natured; friendly

ancestor   (ăn´ sĕs tər)   one who goes before; a person from whom one is descended

animosity   (ăn´ ə mŏs´ ĭ tē)   ill will; hatred

annex   (ăn´ ĕks)   an addition to something

antagonist   (ăn tăg´ ə nĭst)   opponent; foe

antisocial   (ăn tē sō´ shəl)   not getting along well with others

apprehensive   (ăp´ rĭ hĕn´ sĭv)   troubled by fears; uneasy

arduous   (är´ jōō əs)   difficult to do; hard

ascend   (ə sĕnd´)   move upward, climb

ascertain   (ăs´ ər tān´)   to find out for sure

assert   (ə sûrt´)   to declare; to state positively

astrology   (ə strŏl´ ə jē)   a pseudo-science which claims to be able to foretell the future from studying the stars

astronomy   (ə strŏn´ ə mē)   the science of stars and heavenly bodies

atheist   (ā´ thē ĭst)   one who does not believe in God

audacity   (ô das´ ĭ tē)   bold; daring; courage

automaton   (ô tŏm´ ə tŏn)   a person or animal acting in a mechanical way; a robot

avid   (ăv´ ĭd)   very eager; enthusiastic

awe   (ô)   a mixed feeling of reverence, fear; wonder

beckon   (bĕk´ ən)   to summon with a silent gesture

belated   (bĭ lā´ tĭd)   tardy; late

belligerent   (bə lĭj´ ər ənt)   hostile; warlike

beneficial   (bĕn ə fĭsh´ əl)   favorable, helpful

betrayal   (bĭ trā´ əl)   a disloyal or traitorous act

bewitch   (bĭ wĭch´)   to cast a spell over; to charm

bizarre   (bĭ zär´)   odd in manner or appearance; unconventional

boorish   (bōōr´ ish)   rude; awkward; ill-mannered

brazen   (brā´ zən)   shameless; rude

brevity   (brĕv´ ĭ tē)   briefness, shortness; concise expression

brogue   (brōg)   Irish accent

browse   (brouz)   to glance through something in a leisurely way

brusque (brŭsk)   blunt in manner or speech; rude

brutality (brōō tăl´ ĭ tē)   savagery; cruelty

bulge (bŭlj)   to swell

candid (kăn´ dĭd)   honest; direct; straight for-ward; open

cantankerous (kăn tăng´ kər əs)   bad tempered; quarrelsome

capitulate (kə pĭch´ ə lāt´)   to give up; surrender

captive (kăp´ tĭv)   one held as a prisoner

cardinal (kär´ dən əl)   fundamental; principal; chief

caress (kə rĕs´)   an affectionate touch as a kiss; hug

casual (kăzh´ ōō əl)   happens by chance; infor-mal

catapult (kăt´ ə pŭlt)   to shoot as from a sling-shot; to hurl

celebrity (sə lĕb´ rĭ tē)   a famous person

chaos (kā´ ŏs)   great confusion or disorder

chastise (chăs tīz´)   to punish in order to correct

chateau (shă tō´)   a large country house; a French castle

chortle (chôr´ təl)   to chuckle or laugh

clement (clĕm´ ənt)   lenient, mild; merciful

cliff (klĭf)   a high, steep rock

clique (klĭk)   a small, exclusive circle of people

collaborator (kə lăb´ ə rā tər)   a person working together with another

colleague (kŏl´ ēg)   a fellow worker in the same profession

collide (kə līd´)   to crash violently; to come together with an impact

combatant (kŏm´ bə tənt)   a fighter

comely (kəm´ lē)   attractive; pretty; handsome

competent (kŏm´ pī tnt)   able; fit; adequate

complacent (kəm plā´ sənt)   self-satisfied; smug

compose (kəm pōz´)   to create; to make calm

compress (kəm prĕs´)   to press together

concise (kən sīs´)   brief and to the point

condescend (kŏn dĭ sĕnd´)   to act as if another is inferior to you; to deal with others in a supe-rior way

console (kən sōl´)   to comfort; to aid

conspicuously (kən spĭk´ yōō əs ly)   obviously; remarkably

contradict (kŏn trə dĭkt´)   to go against; to op-pose verbally

contrite (kən trīt´)   feeling sorrow for one's sin

cosmopolitan (kŏz mə pŏl´ ə tən)   belonging to the whole world; at home in all countries

courteous (kûr´ tĭ əs)   polite; considerate of others

covet (kŭv´ ĭt)   to desire something that belongs to another

credible (krĕd´ ə bəl)   believable

crest (krĕst)   the top of something, like a wave or ridge

cubicle (kyōō´ bĭ kəl)   a small compartment or room

cumulative (kyōō´ myə lā´ tĭv)   increasing by successive additions; additional

current (kûr´ ənt)   now in progress; at the present time

curt (kûrt)   brief and rude in speech or manner; shortened

dapper (dăp´ ər)   trim; neat; small and active

deception (dĭ sĕp´ shən)   a dishonest or misleading act

decipher (dĭ sī´ fər)   to figure out the meaning

deflate (dĭ flāt´)   to lessen in size, importance; to let air out

deformed (dĭ fôrm´ d)   misshapen

degeneration (dĭ jĕn ə rā´ shən)   deterioration; a worsening condition; a decline

dejected (dĭ jĕk´ tĭd)   low in spirits; depressed

demeanor (dĭ mē´ nər)   outward behavior, conduct

depreciate (dĭ prē shē āt´)   to lessen in value or price

deprivation (dĕp rə vā´ shən)   the act of doing without something

descend (dĭ sĕnd´)   come or go down

desecrate (dĕs´ ĭ krāt)   to violate the sacredness of

desolate (dĕs´ ə lĭt)   lonely; a deserted and barren area

dialogue (dī ə lôg)   conversation with another

dilemma (dĭ lĕm´ ə)   an situation that demands a choice; a problem

disaster (dĭ zăs´ tər)   great harm or damage; sudden misfortune

discern (dĭ sûrn´)   to make out something that is not clear

dismiss (dĭs mĭs´)   to send away, remove; to fire from a job

dissuade (dĭ swäd´)   to change a person's way of thinking or acting

divert (dĭ vûrt´)   to turn aside

domain (dō mān´)   territory under one's control

drudgery (drŭj´ ə rē)   work that is hard or unpleasant

dubious (dōō´ bĕ əs)   uncertain; doubtful

dwindle (dwĭn´ dəl)   to decrease; diminish; shrink

eccentric (ĭk sĕn´ trĭk)   out of the ordinary; unconventional

eclipse (ĭ klĭps´)   cutting off of light; temporary obscurity

ecstasy (ĕk´ stə sē)   a feeling of overpowering joy

edible (ĕd´ ə bəl)   able to be eaten

elapse (ĭ lăps´)   to slip or pass by

elation (ĭ lā´ shən)   high spirits; a strong feeling of joy

eloquence (ĕl´ ə kwəns)   vivid, forceful speech or writing

embellish (ĕm bĕl´ ĭsh)   to decorate; to ad details

emerge (ĭ mûrj´)   to rise out from; to become visible

eminent (ĕm´ ə nənt)   outstanding; noteworthy

emit (ĭ mĭt´)   to send out; to utter

emulate (ĕm´ yə lāt)   to try to equal; imitate

encore (än´ kôr)   a request for an additional performance

engulf (ĕn gŭlf´)   to swallow up; overwhelm

envious (ĕn´ vē əs)   jealousy

epilogue (ĕp´ ə lôg)   a closing section of a novel or play

equilibrium (ē kwə lĭb´ re əm)   a state of balance

equitable (ĕk´ wĭ tə bəl)   fair; just

eternal (ĭ tûr´ nəl)   everlasting; timeless; never changing

eviction (ĭ vĭk´ shən)   the act of putting a tenant out legally; expel

evolution (ĕv ə lōō´ shən)   gradual development; a process of change

exhilarate (ĭg zĭl´ ə rāt)   to refresh; to make very happy

exhort (ĭg zôrt´)   to urge earnestly; encourage

expunge (ĭk spŭnj´)   to blot or wipe out; erase

exquisite (ĭk skwĭz´ ĭt)   very beautiful; charming

extinct (ĭk stĭnkt´)   no longer in existence

exuberant (ĭq zōō´ bər ənt)   lively; high spirited

facade (fə säd´)   the front of a building; a deceptive outward appearance

fathom (făth´ əm)   to understand; comprehend

feign (fān)   to pretend; to give a false appearance

fervent (fûr´ vənt)   showing deep feeling or great emotion

fiasco (fē ăs´ kō)   a complete failure

fiscal (fĭs´ kəl)   relating to financial matters

fissure (fĭsh´ ər)   a long, narrow crack; a deep split

flank (flăngk)   the right or left side of a formation

flout (flout)   to ignore; to show contempt for

fluent (flōō´ ənt)   smooth easy speech

flurry (flûr´ ē)   a sudden gust of wind, rain, or snow; a sudden commotion

forlorn (fôr lôrn´)   miserable; without hope

fortunate (for´ chə nĭt)   lucky; favorable

fragile (frăj´ əl)   easily broken; delicate

frail (frāl)   physically weak, fragile

fraternity (frə tûr´ nĭ tē)   brotherhood; Greek letter college organization

fraud (frôd)   a trick; deception

frigid (frĭj´ ĭd)   extremely cold; stiff and formal

frugal (frōō´ gəl)   not wasteful; economical; cheap

galley (găl´ ē)   a ship's kitchen

garment (gär´ mĕnt)   an article of clothing

gaunt (gônt)   thin and bony

genial (jēn´ yəl)   cheerful; friendly

gesticulate (jăs tik´ yə lāt)   to make gestures for emphasis

ghastly (găst´ lē)   horrible; gruesome; grim

giddy (gĭd´ ē)   dizzy; frivolous

gigantic (jī găn´ tĭk)   huge; enormous; very large

gimmick (gĭm´ ĭk)   a trick

glance (glăns)   to look briefly; a quick glimpse

gorgeous (gôr´ jəs)   beautiful; magnificent

gracious (grā´ shəs)   having or showing kindness

graphic (grăf´ ĭk)   vivid; described in realistic detail

grisly (grĭz´ lē)   terrifying; ghastly

grotesque (grō tĕsk´)   bizarre; distorted

grovel (grŭv´ əl) to act humbly; crawl; cringe

grudge (grŭj) a strong feeling of resentment; ill will

Hades (ha´ dēz) hell; place for the dead

hereditary (hə rĕ´ də tĕr ē) passed down from ancestors

heritage (hĕr´ ĭ tĭj) something handed down from one's ancestors

hideous (hĭd´ ē əs) very ugly; horrible

hierarchy (hī´ ə rär kē) a group of persons or things arranged in order of rank, grade, or class

homely (hōm´ lē) simple; plain; unattractive

horrify (hôr´ ə fī) to shock

humiliate (hyōō mĭl´ ē āt) to lower someone's pride or dignity; to disgrace

hypothetical (hī pə thĕt´ ĭ kəl) assumed; supposed

idiosyncrasy (ĭd ē ō sĭng´ krə sē) a peculiar form of behavior

illusion (ĭ lōō´ zhən) a false idea or misleading appearance or belief

immense (ĭ măns´) very large

impeccable (ĭm pĕk´ ə bəl) without defect or error; flawless

imperative (ĭm pĕr´ ə tĭv) absolutely necessary; urgent

impious (ĭm´ pe əs) lacking reverence for God

implication (ĭm plĭ kā´ shən) something suggested but not stated directly

implore (ĭm plôr´) to beg; to appeal

impose (ĭm pōz´) to force oneself on another

impulse (ĭm´ pŭls) a driving force; push; a sudden urge to act

impunity (ĭm pyōō´ nĭ tē) freedom from punishment

inarticulate (ĭn är tĭk´ yə lĭt) unable to speak clearly

incessant (ĭn sĕs´ ənt) never stopping; constant

inconsequential (ĭn kŏn sĭ kwĕn´ shəl) unimportant

indignant (ĭn dĭg´ nənt) feeling or expressing anger, especially at an unjust action

indolent (ĭn´ də lənt) lazy; idle; disliking work

indomitable (ĭn dŏm´ ĭ tə bəl) unbeatable; unconquerable

indubitably (ĭn dōō´ bĭ tə bə lē) without a doubt; unquestionably

indulgent (ĭn dŭl´ jənt) overly kind or lenient

inert (ĭ nûrt´) slow to move or act

inexplicable (ĭn ĕk splĭ kə bəl) cannot be explained or understood

infectious (ĭn fĕk´ shəs) easily spread; capable of infection

infirm (ĭn fûrm´) weak; feeble

initiate (ĭ nĭsh´ ē āt) to bring into use; to begin

intangible (ĭn tăn´ jə bəl) not able to be touched

intensive (ĭn tĕn´ sĭv) thorough or necessary; concentrated

interim (ĭn´ tər ĭm) time between events

interminable (ĭn tûr´ mə nə bəl) never-ending

interpose (ĭn tər pōz´) to come between; interrupt

intimate (ĭn´ tə mĭt) very private or personal; very familiar

intoxication (ĭn tŏk sĭ kā´ shən) drunkenness

introspective (ĭn trə spĕk´ tĭv) looking into one's own mind, feelings

invalid (ĭn văl´ ĭd) not effective or legal

jeer (jĭr) to shout at in a rude, sarcastic way

jeopardy (jĕp´ ər dē) risk; danger

knack (năk) ability to do something easily

laceration (lăs ə rā´ shən) a jagged tear or wound

ladle (lād´ l) long handled cup-like spoon

lament (lə mĕnt´) to mourn or grieve for

lean (lēn) to tend or favor slightly; to incline

lethargic (lə thär´ jĭk) dull; sluggish; abnormally drowsy

limber (lĭm´ bər) easily bent; moving easily

literate (lĭt´ ər ĭt) educated; able to read and write

loathe (lōth) to feel disgust for; to hate

luminous (lōō´ mə nəs) bright; giving off light

malady (măl´ ə dī) illness; disease

malice (măl´ ĭs) evil intent; ill feeling towards another

malignant (mə lĭg´ nənt) very harmful; having an evil influence

malleable (măl´ ē ə bəl) pliable; easily bent; easily influenced

mansion (măn´ shən) a large, expansive house

marital (măr´ ĭ təl) relating to marriage

martial (mär´ shəl) warlike; bold; of the military

massive (măs´ ĭv) large and heavy; impressive

meager (mē´ gər) not enough; inadequate

melancholy (mĕl´ n kŏl ē) sad; depressed; gloomy

metamorphosis (mĕt ə môr´ fə sĭs) a change from one form to another

migrate (mī´ grāt) to move from one place to another

mingle (mĭn´ gəl) to mix together; combine, blend

mirage (mĭ räzh´) something that appears to be real, but isn't; an illusion

miscreant (mĭs´ krə ənt) a criminal; villain; evil person

mistreatment (mĭs trēt´ mĭnt) cruelty; abuse

mock (mŏk) to ridicule; mimic

modest (mŏd´ ĭst) shy; quiet and humble

modification (mŏd ə fĭ kā´ shən) a partial change in form

monologue (mŏn´ ə lôg) one person speaking

monotony (mə nŏt´ n ē) lack of variety; tiresome; sameness

mortal (môr´ tl) a being who must eventually die

mourn (môrn) to feel or express sorrow for a death or loss

mural (myōōr´ əl) a large picture painted on a wall

mute (myōōt) not speaking; silent

mythical (mĭth´ ĭ kəl) imaginary or fictitious

naive (nä ēv´) unsophisticated; foolishly simple

navigation (năv ə gā´ shən) directing or steering the course of a ship or aircraft

nimble (nĭm´ bəl) moving quickly and lightly

68

nonchalant   (nŏn shə **länt´**)   without enthusiasm; casually indifferent

nutrition   (nōō **trĭsh´** ən)   anything that nourishes; food

oblique   (ō **blēk´**)   indirect; slanting

obliterate   (ə **blĭt´** ə rāt)   to blot out; leaving no trace

oblivious   (ə **blĭv´** ē əs)   forgetful; unaware

obscure   (əb **skyōōr´**)   hard to understand; unknown; vague

obsolete   (ŏb sə **lēt´**)   out of date; no longer in use

odor   (ō´ dər)   smell; aroma

odyssey   (ŏd´ ĭ sē)   any extended wandering or journey

ominous   (ŏm´ ə nəs)   threatening; sinister

opaque   (ō **pāk´**)   not transparent; not reflecting light; hard to understand

oppressive   (ə **prĕs´** ĭv)   hard to put up with; burdensome; overbearing

overwhelming   (ō vər **wĕlm´** ĭng)   overpowering; overcoming completely

pacify   (pǎs´ ə fī)   to make peaceful or calm

palatial   (pə **lā´** shəl)   like a palace; magnificent

pamper   (pām´ pər)   to treat with great kindness

panacea   (pǎn ə **sē´** ə)   a supposed cure for all diseases

pandemonium   (pǎn də **mō´** nē əm)   wild disorder, noise, or confusion

paralysis   (pə **rǎl´** ĭ sĭs)   loss of the power of motion

pauper   (pô´ pər)   an extremely poor person

peer   (pêr)   person of same rank or age

pensive   (pĕn´ sĭv)   thinking deeply; thoughtful

peonage   (pĕ´ ən ĭj)   a person forced into labor to work off a debt; to work as a peon

pertain   (pər **tān´**)   to be appropriate; to refer to

pestilence   (pes´ tə ləns)   a deadly epidemic; disease

phantom   (fǎn´ təm)   an illusion; a ghost

picturesque   (pĭk chə **rĕsk´**)   like a picture; having a natural beauty

pier   (pîr)   a structure over water used as a landing place for boats

pigment   (pĭg´ mənt)   coloring matter in cells and tissues of plants and animals

pilfer   (pĭl´ fər)   to steal something of little value

pious   (pī´ əs)   showing religious devotion

placate   (plā´ kāt)   to pacify; calm down

plague   (plāg)   anything that troubles or torments; a contagious disease

plateau   (plǎ **tō´**)   an elevated area of level land

plausible   (plô´ zə bəl)   seemingly true or reasonable

pliable   (plī´ ə bəl)   easily bent; flexible; easily influenced

ponder   (pŏn´ dər)   to think deeply; deliberate

precise   (prĭ **sīs´**)   accurate; definite

predator   (prĕd´ ə tər)   one who hunts or robs

predestination   (pre dĕs tə **nā´** shən)   the belief that all events have been planned in advance by God

predominate   (prĭ **dŏm´** ə **nāt´**)   to have superiority

prey   (prā)   the hunted

69

progeny (prŏj´ ə ne) children; descendants

prominent (prŏm´ ə nənt) sticking out; noticeable at once

prompt (prŏmpt) quick; without delay

prosperous (prŏs pər əs) enjoying wealth or success

providence (prŏv´ ə dəns) benevolence of God or nature

prudent (prōōd´ nt) sensible; cautious in conduct

punctual (pŭnk´ chōō əl) on time; prompt

purgatory (pûr´ gə tŏr ē) a place of temporary suffering

quarry (kwôr´ ē) something hunted or chased; prey

quirk (kwûrk) a sudden twist, turn; a peculiar behavior

ramble (răm´ bəl) to move about idly; talk or write aimlessly

raucous (rô´ kəs) loud and disorderly

ravine (rā´ vən) a long, deep cut in the earth worn by a stream

reckon (rĕk´ ən) to figure; estimate; assume

reformation (rĕ fər mā´ shən) the act of changing something

refuge (rĕf´ yōōj) a place of safety

refugee (rĕf´ yōō jē) one who flees home or country in search of safety

refute (rĭ fyōōt´) to prove to be wrong or false

rehabilitate (rē hə bĭl´ ĭ tāt) to put back in good condition; to fix up

reign (răn) dominance or power; to rule as a monarch

reminiscence (rĕm ə nĭs´ əns) memory; recollection

renounce (rĭ nouns) to disown; to give up

resolute (rĕz´ ə lōōt) determined; having a firm purpose

respite (rĕs´ pĭt) a delay or postponement; reprieve

reverence (rĕv´ ər əns) a feeling of deep respect

revert (rĭ vûrt´) to go back; return

ricochet (rĭk ə shā´) to rebound off a surface

ridicule (rĭd´ ĭ kyōōl) to make fun of; mock

rove (rōv) to wander about, especially over a large area

ruin (rōō´ ĭn) to harm; to cause the downfall of

ruminate (rōō´ mə nāt) to reflect on; to think about

rural (rŏor´ əl) of or like the country; rustic

saga (sā´ gə) a long story of heroic deeds

sage (sāj) wise; a wise man

salutation (săl yōō tä´ shən) a greeting

sanctity (săngk´ tĭ tē) holiness; sacredness

sanctuary (săngk´ chōō ĕr ĕ) a holy place for worship; a protected place of safety

sarcasm (sär kăz əm) a sharp, mocking remark

scandalous (skăn´ dl əs) shameful, shocking

scant (skănt) not enough; inadequate

scold (skōld) to find fault with; to reprimand

scorch (skôrch) to burn slightly

scrutinize (skrōōt´ n īz´) to examine closely

scrutiny (skrōōt´ n ē) close examination; a long, careful look

sedative (sĕd´ ə tĭv) medicine to soothe or quiet

seethe (sēth) to boil; to be violently agitated

seize (sēz) to grasp suddenly; to capture

seldom (sĕl´ dəm) rarely; not often

sensible (sĕn´ sə bəl) wise; showing good sense

sentimental (sĕn tə mĕn´ tl) having or showing tenderness; emotional

serene (sə rēn´) calm; quiet; undisturbed; peaceful

sinewy (sĭn´ yōō ē) lean and muscular

sinister (sĭn´ ĭ stər) threatening; wicked, evil or dishonest

skeptic (skĕp´ tĭk) one who doubts and questions

slender (slĕn´ dər) long and thin; slim

sludge (slŭj) mud; ooze

sly (slī) clever; crafty; underhanded

smug (smŭg) self-satisfied; complacent

solemn (sŏl´ əm) formal; serious

solicit (sə lĭs´ ĭt) to want to get or obtain

spasm (spăz´ əm) a sudden, involuntary muscle contraction

spectacle (spĕk´ tə kəl) something remarkable to look at

squirm (skwûrm) to twist and turn

stow (stō) to pack or store away

strenuous (strĕn yōō s) requiring great effort or energy

stupor (stōō´ pər) partial or complete loss of sensibility

suave (swäv) smoothly gracious or polite; polished

substantiate (səb stăn´ chē āt) to prove the truth of

subterfuge (sŭb´ tər fyōōj) deception; evasion

subtle (sŭt´ əl) not obvious; difficult to see

succulent (sŭk´ yə lənt) full of juice or sap

sullen (sŭl´ ən) glum; gloomy; threatening

superfluous (sōō pûr´ flōō əs) unnecessary; extra; not needed

supposition (sŭp ə zĭsh´ ən) a theory; a guess

taint (tānt) to spoil; to make morally corrupt

tamper (tăm´ pər) to interfere harmfully

tarry (tăr´ ē) to delay, linger; to stay for a time

taunt (tônt) to insult or mock

tedious (tē´ dē əs) tiresome; boring

teeter (tē´ tər) to walk or move unsteadily

tempest (tĕm´ pĭst) a violent storm; uproar

tenacious (tə nā´ shs) holding on firmly; stubborn

terse (tûrs) free of unnecessary words; concise; short

texture (tĕks´ chər) the feel of a fabric

thrash (thrăsh) to beat; to move violently

tinge (tĭnj) to color slightly; a trace or slight flavor

topical (tŏp´ ĭ kəl) of a particular place; current

torpor (tôr´ pər) sluggishness; slow moving

tranquil (**trăng´** kwĭl) calm; serene; peaceful

transcend (trăn **sĕnd´**) to exceed; to go beyond or over

transit (**trăn´** sĭt) passage through or across

transition (trăn **zĭsh´** ən) the process of changing from one form or state to another

transplant (trăns **plănt´**) to move a living thing from one place to another

treacherous (**trĕch´** ər əs) unreliable; untrustworthy; dangerous

trench (trĕnch) a long, narrow ditch

trifle (**trī´** fəl) something of little value or importance

unanimous (yōō **năn´** ə məs) agreeing completely; acting as one

uncanny (ŭn **kən´** ē) mysterious; strange

unconcern (ŭn kən **sûrn´**) lack of interest

unruly (ŭn **rōō´** lē) disorderly; difficult to control

urban (**ûr´** bən) relating to the city

vague (vāg) not clear; uncertain, hazy

valor (**văl´** ər) courage; fearlessness

varmint (**vär´** mənt) an objectionable person or animal

veer (vër) to turn aside from a course or direction

vehemently (**vē´** ə mənt lĭ) violently; passionately

velocity (və **lŏs´** ĭ tē) rate of speed an object moves

vengeance (**vĕn´** jəns) the act of causing harm to another for the purpose of getting even

ventilate (**vĕn´** t lāt) to circulate fresh air

vex (vĕks) to disturb; annoy

vial (**vī´** əl) a glass container for holding liquids

vile (vīl) disgusting; very bad or distasteful

vindictive (vĭn **dĭk´** tĭv) revengeful; spiteful

vital (**vīt´** l) essential; of great importance

vivacity (vĭ **văs´** ĭ tē) liveliness

void (void) an empty space

wander (**wän´** dĕr) to move about aimlessly; ramble

wary (**wâr´** ē) cautious; careful

waver (**wā´** vər) to swing one way then another

wharf (wôrf) a pier; a dock for boats

whimper (**wĭm´** pər) to cry with low, whining, broken sounds

whimsy (**wĭm´** zē) an odd fancy; an idle notion

whine (hwīn) a low cry; to complain

woe (wō) great sorrow; grief

zestful (**zĕst´** fəl) exciting; stimulating